Options Trading for Beginners

The Complete Guide to Investing and Making Money With Options Trading

Gualtiero Favole

© Copyright 2020 by Gualtiero Favole. All right reserved. The work contained herein has been produced with the intent to provide relevant knowledge and information on the topic on the topic described in the title for entertainment purposes only. While the author has gone to every extent to furnish up to date and true information, no claims can be made as to its accuracy or validity as the author has made no claims to be an expert on this topic. Notwithstanding, the reader is asked to do their own research and consult any subject matter experts they deem necessary to ensure the quality and accuracy of the material presented herein.

This statement is legally binding as deemed by the Committee of Publishers Association and the American Bar Association for the territory of the United States. Other jurisdictions may apply their own legal statutes. Any reproduction, transmission or copying of this material contained in this work without the express written consent of the copyright holder shall be deemed as a copyright violation as per the current legislation in force on the date of publishing and subsequent time thereafter. All additional works derived from this material may be claimed by the holder of this copyright.

The data, depictions, events, descriptions and all other information forthwith are considered to be true, fair and accurate unless the work is expressly described as a work of fiction. Regardless of the nature of this work, the Publisher is exempt from any responsibility of actions taken by the reader in conjunction with this work. The Publisher acknowledges that the reader acts of their own accord and releases the author and Publisher of any responsibility for the observance of tips, advice, counsel, strategies and techniques that may be offered in this volume.

Table of Contents

Introduction 1
Chapter 1: History Of Options Trading .. 3

    Olive Harvest And Thales 4
    Tulip Bulb Mania Of The 17th Century 6
    Brokers And Russell Sage 9

Chapter 2: Basics Of Options 12

    What Are Options? 14
    Options And Its Advantages 17
    Options And Its Disadvantages 19
    Styles Of Options 20
    Exotic Options 21

Chapter 3: Choosing Brokers 25

    Opting For Free Education 25
    Testing The Broker's Customer Service 27
    Ensuring That The Trading Platform Is Simple To Use 28
    Proper Assessment Of Breadth, Costs, And Depth Of Data And Tools 31
    Not Weighing The Price Of Commission Heavily 32
    Trading Platforms 34

Chapter 4: Management Of Risk 36

Opting For A Trade Plan 37
Management Of Risk Using Options Spreads 40
Management Of Risk Using Diversification 43
Management Of Risk Using Options Orders 44
Money Management And Position Sizing . 46

Chapter 5: Covered Calls 49

Basics Of Covered Call 51
How Can You Profit From Covered Calls? . 53
When Is The Right Time To Sell Covered Calls? 53

Chapter 6: Putting Into Use The Collar Strategy 56

Collar Strategy In Detail 57
Break Even Point And Collar Profit Loss ... 59
Example Of Collar 61
Forecasting Market 62

Chapter 7: Call Spreads 64

Bull Call Spread 65
Bear Call Spread 70
Calendar Call Spread 74

Chapter 8: Put Spreads 78

Bear Put Spread 79
Bull Put Spread 85

Chapter 9: Common Mistakes Of Beginners 88

Focusing On OTM Options 89
No Proper Exit Plan 90
Not Being Attentive To Small Gains For The Huge Gains 91
Not Paying Attention To Written Options. 92

Chapter 10: Having The Right Mindset 95

Improving Your Mindset 96

Chapter 11: Psychology Of Trading 102

Quick Decisions 103
Understanding Fear 103
Dealing With Greed 105
Developing Rules 106

Conclusion 107

Introduction

Congratulations on purchasing *Options Trading for Beginners*, and thank you for doing so.

The concept of trading is often regarded as a very complex subject most of the time. But it is nothing like that. All you need is some calculation along with a bit of your intelligence. In this guidebook, you will find all the important aspects of options trading and how to start with the same. There are people who think of options trading as being risky and exotic. Also, those who have a huge bank balance can only invest in options. Well, this notion is completely wrong. You might think, how is this wrong? All your questions related to this 'HOW' will be answered in this guidebook. It does not matter what kind of an investor you are; options trading can turn out to be a superb source of income for anyone. It can provide you with excellent profits while also leveling up the structure of your portfolio.

It does not matter if your starting investment is very low. You can gradually improve the same with the help of options. Whenever there is a market downturn, it can also act as a shield of insurance for you. You will come across some superb strategies along with the basics of options trading that you can use in your portfolio. As soon as you end this book, you will feel like the king of options trading.

Thanks again for choosing this book, make sure to leave a short review on Amazon if you enjoy it, i'd really love to hear your thoughts!

Chapter 1: History Of Options Trading

Many of you might think of options trading as a brand new form of investment in comparison to other forms of traditional investment like buying stocks and shares. The current form of options contract, as we all know today, was first introduced at the time when the Chicago Board Of Option Exchange or CBOE was established. However, the basic form of options trading is believed to be formed and established in ancient Greece, somewhat around the fourth century BC. From that ancient time, options have been reigning in the trading market in several forms until the CBOE was formed in 1973. From that year, options were standardized in a proper way for the first time. That was the time when options trading started gaining market credibility. Let us start with the history of options before we jump to the basics of options trading.

Olive Harvest And Thales

The earliest example related to options that were first recorded was referred to in a historical book written by a Greek Philosopher, Aristotle, in the mid 4th century BC. There are several books written by Aristotle on various subjects, and all his writings are of great historical influence. In his famous book 'Politics,' Aristotle decribed his account with another historical philosopher known as the Thales of Miletus. In that book, it was described how Thales profited from a huge olive harvest. He was an expert in astrology and mathematics. So, he tried to combine all his knowledge that he had on all the subjects to create the very first contract of options. By studying the position of the stars, Thales was able to predict that a huge olive harvest was going to take place in his region. So, he was all set for making some good profits from the predictions he made. He succeeded in recognizing that the demand for olive presses was going to rise. His motive was to corner the entire market.

However, despite all his calculations, Thales was facing difficulty in gathering sufficient funds for owning the olive presses in his area. So, he made a plan of paying all the owners of olive presses a certain amount of money to secure all his rights to use the presses at the correct time of harvesting. When the harvesting time arrived, as he already predicted earlier, the harvest of olives was huge. He then resold his rights that be bought from the owners of olive presses to all those people who were in great need of them. In this way, he was able to make some huge profits from his investment.

Indeed, no form of the term was put into use at that time. Thales was the first one who created the first call option, where he used olive presses as the underlying asset.

Thales paid out all his right; however, it was not for the obligation to use the olive presses at a fixed rate. He was also able to exercise all the options that he had in possession to make a huge profit. All this is the basic principle of calls today. The only difference is that we have various other factors present in the game today. For example, financial instruments and commodities in the place of olive presses to act as an underlying asset.

Tulip Bulb Mania Of The 17th Century

Another great occurrence that can be linked to the history of options trading was a huge event in the 17th century. The event is known as the Tulip Bulb Mania that took place in Holland. At that time, tulips were quite popular in that area. In fact, it was regarded as a status symbol among the Dutch aristocrats. The popularity of tulips spread to the other parts of the world as well, along with Europe. All this craze for tulips resulted in a vast demand for tulip bulbs that gradually increased with passing time. However, by this time, calls and puts already got implemented in several markets, mainly because of hedging.

For example, the growers of tulips would purchase puts to safeguard the profits they make if there is a downfall in the rates of tulip bulbs suddenly. The tulip wholesalers opted for buying calls to safeguard themselves from the huge risk of rising rates of tulip bulbs. But all the contracts that were being used at that time were not that developed like today. Also, the market of options was not formal. In the 1630s, the overall demand of tulip bulbs skyrocketed. That lead to an increase in the price of bulbs than the actual value. The contracts of options for the price of bulbs also went up. As a result, a new market developed for dealing with all such contracts that permitted any person to speculate on the overall market of tulip bulbs. Most of the families in Holland opted for heavy investments in all such contracts. They either used up all their savings or by mortgaging their assets, such as property.

The price of tulip bulbs went up. However, it could only keep increasing until the time the tulip bulbs opened. The overall price of the tulip market increased to the point that it was of unsustainable nature. The tulip buyers disappeared from the market as the prices crashed heavily. Ordinary people lost everything they invested. The Dutch economy went into state of recession. As the options market was completely unregulated, there was no possible way for investors to fulfill the options contract obligations. All this created a bad name of options all over the world.

Brokers And Russell Sage

Some noteworthy development was brought forward in the history of options by Russell Sage, an American financer. During the later phase of the 19th century, he started developing calls and puts that could be easily traded in the U.S. over the counter. But no formal nature of the market was still available. However, Sage still opted for the development of an activity that is often regarded as a great breakthrough in the options trading market. Russell Sage was the first individual who developed a pricing relationship between the price of options, the price of underlying assets, and the interest rates. During the latter half of the 18th century, brokers and dealers started placing advertisements to get the attention of buyers and sellers of contracts with the aim of deal brokering.

The primary idea was to create a link between the interested customers and a definite broker to either buy calls or puts on any specific stock.

The options market was continuously being regulated by the brokers only with the trading of contracts over the counter. The market was still illiquid, with only limited activity at this point. Some regulations were brought into the picture by the Securities And Exchange Commission. However, the scale of trading was not progressing, which was noticeable by the late 1960s. In 1968, a significant downfall was noticed in the Chicago trade board in the trading of commodities. Thus, the organization started searching for some brand new ways to develop the business. In the year 1973, the CBOE took up the venture of trading. The options contracts were standardized in the proper way for the very first time. Also, a fair marketplace was developed for trading options. The

Options Clearing Corporation was also established at that time to take care of centralized clearing. It also made sure that the options contracts were fulfilled properly. After all this, options trading was taken to be legitimate.

Chapter 2: Basics Of Options

Before you start with trading, there are several important things that you will have to be aware of. In this chapter, you will find everything related to the basics of options trading. Indeed, there is a wide range of options that are available for investing, and also it comes with various types of financial instruments to accomplish all your goals of making profits. One of the primary tools related to finance is options. Options are very versatile in nature, along with being dynamic than stocks. You might have the question in your mind that how are options more dynamic than stocks? Well, the answer is that in the sector of stocks, you will get only two proper ways of making profits or money.

One is the long one, and the other is the short one. Following the long way, you will have to buy a stock and also wait for a very long time for the value of the stocks to go up. If you want to make some profit, you sell the same. In the short way, you will have to sell some of the shares of a company and then purchase the same shares at a lower price at a later stage. If you opt for options, there are several ways in which you can make some potential profits. You will get the chance to trade options not only on stocks but also on currencies, commodities, and various other indices. The majority of new traders opt for the market of stocks without gaining any kind of experience and education prior to investment. So, you will have to get some proper knowledge to make some good profits from the majority of your investments.

What Are Options?

Options are like any other instruments of finance. The majority of people refer to options as contracts. It is because when someone buys options, they actually gain all the right for trading the underlying assets related to that option within a particular date and also at a specific price. However, there is no fixed obligation for you to do so. In short, options are a mere form of security, just like a bond or stock. When it comes to the arena of options trading, you will come across two definite types of options contracts:

- **Call options:** You will get the chance of purchasing all the related underlying assets within a fixed time frame and at a specific rate.

- **Put options:** You will get the chance to sell all the related underlying assets within a fixed time frame and at a specific rate.

No matter which kind of option you opt for, both the contracts come with a predetermined selling or buying rate. The selling or buying price is known as the strike price. The date of expiry is the date when the overall validity of options comes to an end. After the expiry date, the option contract will turn out to be valueless. Before the contract reaches the expiry date, you will have all the right to hand over the same to someone else to make a nice profit. However, you will have to keep in mind that as there is time decay, the contract will be gradually losing its true value as it nears the expiry date. Every third Friday of any month is very important for any trader as in the majority of cases, Saturday is regarded as the expiry date that comes right next to the third Friday. The expiry date for the contract of options might vary. For example, the expiry date might turn out to be as long as a year for some options, whereas some of the options might have their expiry date at a very short term, like one week. In general, the traded options last for about one month to three months.

The component that is used for determining the price of the options contract is known as premium. The condition of the market will keep affecting the value of the premium constantly. It also depends on the overall performance of the underlying security. The time value, when added up with the intrinsic value, will provide you with the premium value. The time value will depend on the total time that is left before the expiry date. As already mentioned before, the more time left, the greater will be the time value. If you want to sell out an option, you will have to deduct the profit from the premium.

Options And Its Advantages

In the world of options trading, there are several advantages. Let's have a look at them.

- **Lesser financial commitment:** As you purchase some shares, you will have to give in a large amount of money. However, when it comes to options trading, the overall amount required for buying an option is comparatively less in comparison to the trading of stocks.

- **Lesser buyer pitfalls:** No matter if you want to buy a call option or a put option, you will have to continuously keep up with the trade. In case you make some incorrect decisions while figuring out the overall time frame, you will only lose the money that you have already paid to get the contract along with the trading fees.

- **More flexibility:** There are several strategies open right in front of the investors that they can effectively apply before the expiry date. They will get the chance to enhance their portfolio after exercising the contract and then purchasing the shares. They will also get the chance to sell either some or an entire portion of the shares that they bought or possess.

- **Determining the price of stock:** While discussing options trading, you, as the investor, will get the power to fix the price of the stock. In short, right before the expiry date, you will get the chance to sell or buy the stock at the determined strike price during any time that has been set.

Options And Its Disadvantages

Just like anything else in this world, options trading also includes some disadvantages.

- **Risk of great loss for all the sellers:** In the last section, we discussed that the buyer would not make any loss, regardless of what happens. However, when it comes to the aspect of the seller, they might face some huge losses. It is primarily because of the fact that when an investor writes calls or puts, they automatically come under the terms of trading the shares. It does not even depend on the market condition before the expiry date.

- **Decay of time:** Another great disadvantage of options trading is time decay. The closer an option gets to the date of expiry, the more will be the value of the loss. When the option reaches the expiry date, it will have zero value unless the option is being exercised in-the-money.

- **Constrained time:** In general, options are bound to play for the short term. So, all the investors will look out for movements in the short-term price to use the same in their favor. All these movements are required to take place within a fixed period of a few weeks to a few months. In fact, it might take place within a few days sometimes.

Styles Of Options

We have already discussed the basic types of options in the earlier sections. There are other option styles as well that we will learn about in this section. Most of the options that you will purchase will fall under any of these categories:

American Options or European Options. Both of these are often referred to as vanilla options.

American Options

In this, you will get the chance to exercise the options any time before the expiry date. The majority of options on stocks and equity fall under this. All such contracts are the ones that can be traded for future exchanges.

European Options

Such options can be exercised on the expiry date only that has already been defined in the options contract. Such options are most often traded in the over-the-counter market.

Exotic Options

There are some option styles that are somewhat exotic than others.

Bermuda Options

Such options lie between American and European options. The options can be exercised on more than one date during the contract period.

Barrier Options

Such options are of completely different nature than the other types of options. In this, to pay off the price of the underlying security, it has to cross a particular level. They can be either a pull or a call option. Options of this nature are of four types:

- **Down-and-out:** It offers the holder every right but without any obligation to sell or purchase the shares of the underlying assets at a fixed strike price that has been predetermined until the price of the asset does not go below a certain barrier during the lifespan of the option. Once the asset price gets below the barrier, there will be no value of the option.

- **Down-and-in:** It is the complete opposite of the down-and-out option. It will carry a value only if the price of the underlying asset goes below a certain barrier during the lifespan of any option.

- **Up-and-out:** It is quite similar to the down-and-out option. The only difference between these two is the placement of the barrier. The options will be knocked out when the price of the underlying asset goes above the determined barrier.

- **Up-and-in:** It is quite similar to the down-and-in option. In this, the barrier placement is made above the underlying asset's current price. The option will be regarded as valid only when the underlying asset's price touches the determined barrier before expiration.

Chapter 3: Choosing Brokers

Options trading, at times, might take the shape of a complicated game. However, when you opt for a broker for your options with proper knowledge and care, you can be the master of the game quite easily. You will gain knowledge about conducting several types of research, tracking the positions, and placing trades. But there are some other essential things that you will have to take care of to find the perfect broker according to your needs.

Opting For Free Education

In case you are a beginner in the world of options trading or if you are willing to enhance all your trading strategies, looking out for a broker who can provide you with education regarding the same is essential. Education of this type can come in several forms:

- Online courses related to options trading
- Live or recorded webinars
- Face to face training
- Over the phone or online guidance

It is quite an effective idea to always be in the student-driver mode. Try to take in as much education as you can. If any broker provides you with a simulated version of their trading platform, you can also take a test drive of the entire process with the help of paper trading account. All this will help you to get a hold of everything before you start giving in your real money online.

Testing The Broker's Customer Service

Great and reliable customer service is essential if you are new to the trading world. A broker can be regarded as perfect when proper customer service is being provided. It is necessary for all those who are trying to opt for a new broker or are trying to get into the world of complex trades for which they need the help. First, you will have to start with the type of contact that you would like. Online live chat or email? Over the phone support? Is there any 24*7 service available for all sorts of technical glitches? Is the service available only on weekends? What kind of representative would you like to contact to answer all your queries related to your account?

The best thing that can be done on your part is to reach out to customer service and ask questions of your concern before you opt for applying for an account. All this will provide you with the necessary help to properly assess the caliber of the service. You can check whether the provided answers are satisfactory or if the response time is decent or not. The overall quality of a broker can be very easily assessed by the kind of customer service provided by them. Also, to be double sure, you can check out reviews of customer service online.

Ensuring That The Trading Platform Is Simple To Use

The platforms for options trading can be found in all types of shapes and sizes. The trading platforms can be desktop or online, web-based or software-based, have multiple platforms for providing basic and advanced training, offer full/partial mobile functionality, or also a mixture of everything. You can start checking by visiting the broker website first. Try to find any guided tour of the platform or of the tools. Screenshots and video tutorials can also offer some functionality. However, trying out any simulated trading platform of the broker, if any is being offered, can help you gain the best knowledge regarding whether the broker is suitable for your use or not. Also, there are some other important things that you will have to consider.

- Is the overall design of the trading platform user-friendly? Are you required to hunt for the tools and things that you will need to trade?

- How easy is it to place any trade on the broker's platform?

- Is the trading platform capable and suitable for meeting all your needs? For example, setting alerts relying on any specific criteria or allowing you fill up a trade ticket in much advance to submit at a later time.

- Will you need mobile access for the full-service suite as you travel? Will a pared-down version of the trading platform be enough for you?

- How fast are the orders executed on the website? Is the broker's website reliable? All of this needs to be at the top of the priority list if your game is to enter and exit the positions quickly.

- Do you need to pay any monthly or annual fee for the trading platform? If yes, is there any possible way of waiving that fee? For example, by maintaining a minimum balance in your account or by opting for a certain number of trades within a specified period?

Proper Assessment Of Breadth, Costs, And Depth Of Data And Tools

Data and research are two things that are always regarded as the lifeblood of an options trader. There are some basic things that you will have to take care of.

- A feed of quotes that is frequently updated

- Basic type of charting to help you select the points of entry and exit

- Screening tools

- The ability to properly analyze the reward nature along with trade risks

If you are trying to opt for an advanced nature of trading, your strategies will need deeper trade modeling, along with analytical tools. All such tools include real-time market data from several providers, customizable types of screeners, and the capability of testing, developing, tracking, and back-testing trading strategies. Try to ensure whether the fancy tools are going to cost you extra. For instance, there are several brokers who can provide you with delayed quotes without any extra cost, lagging behind the market data by twenty minutes, but charges extra for real-time updated feed. Similarly, there are certain tools that are of expert level and are available to those customers only who can meet certain monthly or quarterly trading activity.

Not Weighing The Price Of Commission Heavily

As commissions can give you the chance to compare other brokers side-by-side, they are the primary things that most traders search for before picking a proper broker. You will have to regard certain things related to commissions charged by a broker.

- There are two primary components that determine the commission of options trading. They are base rate and per-contract fee. It is similar to the trading commission that an investor has to pay at the time of purchasing a stock.

- Some brokers also couple the per-contract fee and the trading commission within one single flat fee.

- There are brokers who provide discounted commissions depending on several things like frequency of trading, trading volume, and average maintained balance in the account.

In case you are a beginner or completely new to the trading world, or you just use the strategies rarely, a broker who offers one flat trading rate or the one that comes with no form of commission will be the best choice for you.

Trading Platforms

If you want to earn some good profits, opting for the perfect trading platform is very important. Here are some trading platforms that you can use effectively for a seamless trading experience.

Tastyworks

If you are a frequent trader, this platform can turn out to be your best companion. It comes with several tools that will offer you probability, liquidity, and volatility. Opening up a trading account on this platform is seamless. After you have created your account successfully, you will have to download the trading platform. Before trading, you can try out the different tools for getting a hold of the same. The cost per leg on this platform is $0. The cost will be $1 for each leg for opening a position, where the maximum can be $10 for each leg. Closing the position will cost $0.

Ally Invest

The best aspect of this platform is its low-cost brokerage. Also, there is no need to maintain a minimum account balance. Ally Invest supports the functioning of this platform. You can place orders on this platform within seconds. You can also modify all your settings, opt for technical analysis, and view necessary charts.

E*Trade

E* Trade's platform is the most advanced of all that can provide you with all your required tools. The per-contract commission here is $0.65. If you place more than 30 trades in a single quarter, the commission will be $0.50 for each contract. If the price of the contract is equal to or less than $0.10, any kind of fee is waived off.

Chapter 4: Management Of Risk

A very important thing in the game of options trading is properly managing the capital and exposure to risk. Indeed, risk can be easily avoided in all forms of investment, so risk exposure is not regarded as such a problem. The key here is to manage the risk funds effectively and ensure that you are totally comfortable with the level of risk you will take. You will also need to ensure that you are not exposing the capital and yourself to any form of unsustainable losses. All of this also applies to the management of money. You are needed to start trading by only using that amount of capital that you can afford to lose without overstretching your capabilities. As effective management of risk and money is crucial for successful options trading, you will have to understand the subject properly. You will be gaining all forms of knowledge and some methods in this chapter that will help you manage risk exposure and control the trading budget.

Opting For A Trade Plan

One of the important aspects in the world of trading is to have in possession a proper trading plan that comes with all the required guidelines and parameters for all sorts of trading activities. The main usage of having a trading plan is to provide you with the necessary help to manage risk exposure and your money. The plan of trading that you are going to design for yourself needs to have every possible detail about the trade – starting from the risk level that you are capable of taking to the total amount that you can put into use. As you start trading by following the plan and set up your mind to use that amount of money that you can truly invest in setting up trading of options, you will be able to stay safe from the greatest mistake. The mistake is to put into use cared money.

When you enter the ring of trading with that amount of money that you cannot afford to lose, or you have kept it aside for fulfilling something else, you will have lesser chances of going for any kind of rational decision in your trades. It is true that it is hard to remove any kind of emotions involved in options trading. You will have to be focused as much as you can on those things that you tend to do, along with the reason behind doing the same. As you permit emotions to take over all the control, the chances are high that you will easily lose all the concentration. You might also start behaving irrationally. It can make you chase all your losses from the past trades that went bad or just make all those transactions that you would not have opted for usually. If you keep following the set plan and use the determined capital, you will get the chance to keep all your irrational emotions under your control.

You will also have to adhere to the level of risk that you have already included in your plan. If you want to opt for trades that come with lower risk only, there is no proper reason to try to expose yourself to all those trades that come with higher risk. You might find it quite tempting at times, only because you have experienced a very small amount of loss till now. It might also happen if you try to fix all your losses or when you have done great with any of your low-risk trades. Now, all you are willing to do is enhance the profit level as quickly as possible. But if you have already planned to make or get involved in trades of low risk only, there has to be some reason for doing so. There is nothing good in pushing yourself out from the comfort zone only because of your emotional reasons, as already discussed before.

There are useful ways in which you can manage risks in options trading.

Management Of Risk Using Options Spreads

One of the most effective and strong tools that can be found in options trading is options spreads. It is nothing but when you begin combining more than a single position on the options contracts, which is based on the same underlying asset to create an overall trading position. For example, if you purchase money calls on some specific stock and then opt for writing cheaper out-of-the-money calls once again on a similar stock, you will be creating an option spread called bull call spread. Purchasing in calls indicates that you will get the chance to profit something if the underlying stock value goes up. However, you will lose something or all the money that you have already spent in purchasing them if the underlying stock value does not rise. As you write calls on the same stock, you will get control of some of the starting costs. In this way, you will get the chance to reduce the money that you might lose.

Every strategy of options trading includes using spreads. Spreads can provide you with a great way to manage the risks. You can start using them to reduce the upfront costs of entering positions. You will also be able to reduce the money that you might lose, just like the example of a bull call spread as discussed above. In short, you can get the power to reduce all forms of profits that you might make, along with reducing the overall risk percentage. Spreads can be used to reduce all forms of risks that can be found while entering any short position. For example, if you decide to write puts on a specific stock, you will be able to get a payment upfront just for writing the options. However, you will also increase your exposure to all forms of potential losses in case the stock tends to decline the value. If you opt for purchasing cheaper out of money puts, you will have to put into use a part of the upfront payment.

You can get the chance of preventing any kind of potential loss that might be caused by any decline in the stock. The spread of this type is called a bull put spread. After you have checked both the examples, you can find that it is possible to get into positions where you have got the chance to still gain some amount of profit if the stock price moves in the correct direction. However, you will be able to limit all your losses if the stock price starts going against you. It is the primary reason why traders try to use spreads so often for trading options. They can act as great devices to manage risks effectively.

Management Of Risk Using Diversification

Diversification is another effective technique of managing risks that is widely used today by all investors who are trying to build up their portfolio of stocks by using the idea of hold and buy. The basic functioning of the technique of diversification is to properly spread all the investments over several companies and sectors to create a balanced nature of portfolio. The concept of putting an excessive amount of money into one particular company or sector is avoided. When you have a portfolio of diversified nature, you will have fewer chances to get exposed to any kind of risk than a portfolio built up with only one type of investment. When it comes to the game of options trading, diversification is not considered to be that important. However, it has still got some uses that can help in diversification in several ways.

The principle of functioning remains the same more or less; you would not want to direct an excessive amount of capital for one particular investment only. You can use diversification in options trading in various methods. You can begin diversifying by using a wide collection of strategies, trading a number of options that rely on several types of underlying assets, and opting for trading several types of options. In short, the primary idea of diversification is to let you make profits in several ways. You will not need to rely completely only on one particular outcome for all your trades to be a success.

Management Of Risk Using Options Orders

A simple way of risk management is to utilize several ranges of various order types that you can place. Along with the four primary order types that can be used for opening and closing positions, there are some other types of orders that you can place. Most of such orders can help you to properly manage the risks involved. For instance, a general type of market order will get filled up at the best price right at the time of execution. It is the most generic way of selling and purchasing options. However, in a market that is volatile in nature, all the orders might tend to get filled up at a price point that is either higher or lower than you want them to be. By utilizing limit orders, where you can get the power of setting up the minimum and maximum prices at which your concerned order can be filled, you can avoid purchasing or selling at prices that are not of favorable nature.

Also, there are orders that you can use to automate the task of exiting a position. It does not matter whether that is to lower the losses on any specific trade that failed to function properly for you or to lock in the probable profits you have already made. By utilizing orders like a market stop order, trailing stop order, or limit stop order, you will get the power to effectively control your point of exit at any position. You will also be able to limit the risk percentage to which you are exposed to on the trades that you want to make.

Money Management And Position Sizing

Money management is directly linked to risk management. Both of these two are essential on the same scale. You will have a certain amount of money that you can use. So, it is of great importance to have proper control on the capital budget. You will have to make sure that you do not just end up losing all you have and then placing yourself in a suffocating position where you can no longer get involved in trading. The perfect way of money management that you already have in your hand is by opting for the simple concept of position sizing. It involves the process of determining the part of the capital that you have in hand to be used in entering a particular position.

To make position sizing the most effective, you will have to take care of the amount of money you truly want to invest in any possible form of trade concerning the percentage of the entire capital investment. Many people also regard the position to be somewhat similar to that of diversification in several aspects. By deciding to use up a small percentage of the in-hand capital in one form of trade, it will be foolish of you to depend only on one specific outcome. Even all the professional traders who are quite successful in the market will make the mistake of making trades that might result badly with time. The key over here is to ensure that the bad trades cannot affect you much worse.

For instance, if you make up your mind to use 50% of the total in-hand capital in one trade only, and it results in a complete loss, you will lose a great amount of funds that you have. In place of doing that, try to use 12% - 15% of your capital for each trade. Even if you make recurring losses, the losses will not be able to destroy you.

Chapter 5: Covered Calls

The covered call is quite a common strategy that can be used in options trading. It can be used when you have some stocks in your possession. You can sell at-the-money or out-of-the-money calls in the same proportion to the shares in hand. For example, you have 1000 shares of DEF stock. You will be able to sell a maximum of 10 calls in a covered call transaction. A buy-write, also known as call write, is a useful strategy that belongs to the covered call strategy. In this, the purchasing of stocks and selling out of options will be a part of the same transaction. The platform of trading that you are going to use might have the ability to execute a buy-write order. For instance, the selling price of any call is set at $2, and the stock is traded at a price of

$100, you will be able to enter one single order to execute the entire transaction at a price of $98 or even more than that.

When you decide to enter a limit order in this manner, you will not be able to execute on one side of the entire transaction unless the other side is also executed. As you sell out a covered call, you will get the chance to profit from three basic sources:

- Premium of the option
- Increase in the price of the underlying asset
- Stock dividends

An option position is generally regarded as being covered, for this purpose, when an offsetting is available in the opposite position of the market, for example, long stock. You will have to note that one downside of a covered call is its incapability to earn interest on all those proceeds that are used up to purchase the stocks. However, you will be entitled to get the dividends if you own the stocks. A covered option comes with various risks. For instance, if a trader is long 100 shares of a certain stock that is also being traded at a rate of $100 for each share, and he decides to sell one call at $2 ($200). At that time, the stock price goes up to $50 for each share; the trader will lose $50,000 in total long stock. The trader will receive a premium that will function as a consolation gift only.

Basics Of Covered Call

A covered call can serve as the hedge of either short-term or any position of long stock. It lets the investors to get their income through the received premium after writing any option. But the investor will forfeit all the gains from the stocks if the price of the stock goes above the option's strike price. In case the buyer makes up his mind to exercise an option, the investors will have to provide a total of 100 shares at the option's strike price. The covered call strategy will not be useful for any investor who is bullish or bearish. If an investor is excessively bullish, they will tend not to sell out the price and try to hold back the overall stock.

The profit will be provided by the option on the entire stock, which might lower the entire profit from the trade if the price of the stock goes up. Just like that, when an investor is excessively bearish in nature, they might tend to sell off all their stocks. It is because the premium that the investor will receive for selling out a call will help to offset the entire loss on that particular stock if the price of the stock goes down.

How Can You Profit From Covered Calls?

The buyer will pay the call option seller a premium to get the complete right to purchase the shares or contracts at a price determined already. The premium is nothing but the cash fee, which is paid out on the day when an option is sold. It is also the amount of money that the seller will keep, no matter if the option is exercised or not.

When Is The Right Time To Sell Covered Calls?

As you decide to sell out a covered call, you will get the payment in exchange for leaving a position that might rise in the future. For example, you purchase stocks of DEF at $50 for each share with the belief that it might go up to $60 within a period of 365 days. You might also have the urge to sell out the same at a rate of $55 after a period of 6 months. All of this can easily bring in a short-term profit. In such a case, selling the covered calls on any position might turn out to be a superb strategy. The stock options chain will show that selling an option that is six months old for $55 will cost the buyer a premium of $4 for each share. You will have the choice to sell the option against all your shares, which you have bought for $50 previously, with the hope that you can sell the same, next year, at $60.

Writing this particular call option will result in the creation of an obligation to sell out all the shares at a price of $55 within a period of six months if the price of the underlying asset reaches the same level. You will get the opportunity to keep the premium of $4, along with $55 from the selling shares. So, the total amount will be $59 or a return of 18% within six months. On the other side, you will face a loss of $10 on the position if the stock price comes down to $40. But you will still have the chance to keep the premium of $4 that you will get after you sell out a call option. In this very way, you will be able to lower the overall loss from $10 to $6 for each share. Selling covered calls can help you in offsetting the downside risk or even add up to the upside return, taking along the premium in exchange for any rise in the future above the strike price of the option in addition to the premium.

Chapter 6: Putting Into Use The Collar Strategy

Collar, also known as the hedge wrapper, is a well-known options trading strategy that is most often implemented by investors to protect themselves from huge losses. However, you will also need to keep in mind that it can limit huge gains. As an effective investor, you will get the chance to create a collar position by simply getting an out-of-the-money put option and selling out an out-of-the-money call. The put will protect you if, in any case, the price of the stock tends to go down. As you sell out the call options, you will get the income, and it will also let you earn some profit on that stock, which is limited to the call option's strike price. You cannot earn more than that.

Collar Strategy In Detail

Any investor can decide to execute a collar whenever they have in possession a long-term stock that has not returned any kind of substantial gains or profits. Also, an investor might decide to use the strategy of the collar if they are sure regarding the stock in the long run; however, they are not sure of the prospects in the short-term. To protect the profits from any kind of downwards movement of the stock, the strategy of collar can be successfully implemented. The best-case scenario for an investor will be when the underlying asset's overall price is also the same as the strike price of the call option that has been sold out before the expiration date. The strategy of the collar is composed of two varying strategies: one is the protective put, and the other is the covered call. We have already discussed covered call in the last chapter. A protective put or married put includes staying with an option of put, along with the underlying securities. A covered call includes being short of a call option and also being long for the securities.

The purchasing of an out-of-the-money put option is everything that can help an investor with the necessary protection from any form of potential downfall in the stock price. Selling out a call option of out-of-the-money type will help in the generation of premiums that have already been paid while purchasing the put. Both call and put will have to be of the same expiry month, along with the same contract numbers. The put that has been bought will require having a strike price, which is much lower than the current stock's market price. The call that is being sold out will require a strike price much above the current stock's market price. In fact, the trade will have to be developed for little or zero out-of-the-pocket cost in case you decide to select the respective strike price that is at an equal distance from the present price of the owned stock. As they will be taking a risk by significantly sacrificing all their gains from the stocks above the covered call's strike price, the collar strategy is not a good choice for those investors who are excessively bullish on their stocks.

Break Even Point And Collar Profit Loss

The break even point or BEP of any investor on this strategy is the sum total of all the premium that he has received and also been paid for the call option or put option added or subtracted to/from the purchase price of all the underlying securities relying on whether there is debit/credit. The net credit can be determined when the premiums that have been received are more than the overall premiums that have been paid. The net debit can be determined when the total premiums paid are more than the received premium.

BEP = Underlying asset purchase price + Total debit

BEP = Underlying asset purchase price − Total credit

The overall profit from the collar is equal to the call's strike price minus the stock purchase price per share of the underlying asset. The options cost, whether debit or credit, will be the dividend. The maximum loss will be the purchasing rate of the underlying asset minus the strike price of the put. The option cost will be factored in after that.

Maximum profit = (Call strike price − Net put/Call premiums) − Stock purchase price

Maximum loss = Stock purchase price − (Put strike price − Net put/Call premiums)

Example Of Collar

Suppose you are a trader who is long of XYZ stock by 1000 shares at a fixed price of $80 for each share. The current trading price of the stock is $87 per share. You decide to temporarily hedge your position as there is an increase in the trading market's overall volatility. You purchase 10 puts (one option contract is equal to 100 shares) with the strike price of $77. You sell out 10 calls with the strike price of $97. Your cost for collar implementation (sell the call at $87 and purchase the put at $77) will be a debit of $1.50 for each share.

BEP = $80 + $1.50 = $81.50 each share

The maximum profit that you can earn over here is $15,500 or 10 options contracts x 100 shares x (($80 − ($97 - $1.50)). It will happen if the stock price goes to $97 or even more than that. The maximum loss that you might face is

$4,500 or 10 x 100 x (($77 - $1.50) - $80). It will happen if the stock price goes to $77 or even less than that.

Forecasting Market

Perfect market forecast for collar strategy depends on the purchasing time of the stock, which is also relative to the option's entry positions. It also depends on the willingness of a trader to sell the stock. If any collar position is established by first acquiring the shares, there will be a need for a 2-part forecast. The forecast will have to be entirely neutral from bullish. There is a great need for a proper reason to limit the risks. On the contrary, when a collar is developed to protect any pre-existing holding on a stock, there will be two probable scenarios. The short-term forecast might turn out to be bearish, and the long-term forecast can be bullish. Secondly, the trader might get close to the target selling price of the concerned stock.

Are you enjoying this book? If so, i'd be really happy if you could leave a short review on Amazon, it means a lot to me! Thank you!

Chapter 7: Call Spreads

In call spread, you do not have to develop a stock position. In place of that, you will get the chance to play one strike price against the other. The only disadvantage of this is that you will require having a definite bias of the market. So, they are not completely market neutral from the perspective of a strategy. The inevitable truth is that none of the strategies that are available today is 100% market neutral. But, from the perspective of risk, they can easily insulate you from the sudden movements of the market. That is why it is essential to get to know about all such strategies in detail. Let us have a look at the functioning of call spreads.

Bull Call Spread

The bull call spread will assume that you possess a bullish view on the overall market based on technical analysis. The best part about this very strategy is that it can be very easily adjusted, similar to a collar. However, there is no requirement to establish a long stock position. Indeed, all strategies related to spread come along with the inherent advantage. The strategy of bull call spread can work the best in markets that have been titled as bullish, but in actuality, it is not so. What I am trying to say is that the market often heads in one direction; however, you will notice that it drifts about, diving much often as it rises above with a very small push upwards.

See-saw movement of this sort is a perfect thing for a bull call spread. It can even work in strong bull markets. But personally, I would suggest you to go long on a call for capturing the entire movement. You will have to remember that strong bullish movements of this type tend to happen very rarely. So, you will have to decide and choose with proper care. Let us dive deeper into the functioning of this strategy.

Execution

The bull call spread comes along with two legs:

- A long in or at-the-money call
- A short out-of-the-money call

The main generator of profit in this strategy is the long call. It is all that will capture the stocks' upward movement. It will allow you to earn an increased premium through the enhanced intrinsic value of the concerned option. The short call will be your profit goal effectively or might be a little beyond that. It will increase your total profit along with your earn income from the very premium after writing it. Let us see how the math actually works by taking the example of the AMZN. The market price is set at $1833.51. So, for establishing the first leg of the trade, you will have to choose an at the money or in the money option from the contracts of the near month. The closest that is possible to get is 1835, which is offered out at $63.65 for each share.

Now, what would be the correct target price? Well, it will depend on the way you will be reading the market. If it is going sideways, with a little bit of bullish title, placing the target right at the range boundary will be the best idea. Indeed, your short call will have to be much beyond this very limit. Let's assume our target is set at $1862. It will make writing the strike call at 1865 a great option. The premium that you can get for writing the option will be $44.55 for each share. How does the math work?

Trade entry cost = Long call cost − Short call premium = 63.65 − 44.55 = $19.10 each share

Maximum profit = Short call's strike price − Strike price of long call = 1865 − 1835 =$30 each share

Your trade entry will be the maximum possible loss as if the stock price goes down, as it might be the worst-case scenario, your long call will expire worthless. You will get the chance to keep the entire premium from the short call. Your maximum profit will be capped by the short call's strike price. There is nothing that you need to be worried about the moving of short calls into the money. It is primarily because you will have the lower long call covering this very position. In such a case, you will simply need to exercise the lower call and also use the same to fulfill the exercise of the higher call. The ratio of reward to risk for this particular example will be quite decent, if not amazing.

You will have to note that this very strategy takes full advantage of the non-committal or sluggish markets with a little bullish tilt towards them. In all such markets, a trader who is directional in nature will have a high chance of getting wiped out.

Adjustment

It is actually possible to adjust the bull call spread. Also, all of this will depend on your level of confidence regarding your analysis. The adjustment over here is quite similar to that of the collar. First, you will have to cover a short call position for earning a profit, as the premium might decrease. Secondly, you close out a long call for a loss as it is now going to be out of the money. After all the things are set equal, the long call loss will be offset by the profit that you will get from closing a short call. So, you are still in trade till now. You can reestablish a long call right from a new market level and can determine whether you want to maintain the same target price or just change it.

Bear Call Spread

Just like the bull call spread strategy takes full advantage of the sluggish bull markets, this strategy takes advantage of the sluggish bear markets. The perfect time to put both the strategies into action is right towards the end, where the participation of a counter trend is getting higher by every minute. The market will move into a distributive or accumulative phase to prepare for the trend change. All this happens to be the real market state for the majority of the part. So, you can be assured that both strategies can work great for you. The strategy of bear call spread can also work in a sideways market. In this, the best place to implement is near the topmost end of the sideways range. Let us dive deeper into the execution of this strategy.

Execution

The bear call spread comes with two proper legs:

- A near the money or at the money short call
- A long call of out of the money

The main instrument for earning profit is the short call, which will take advantage of the decreasing price as the long call caps the downside. The main factor of earning in this trade will be the premium that you can earn on writing a short call. Just like the bull call, the maximum loss and profit are capped. All this will provide you with a superb view of the trade probabilities right off your bat. Let us find out how this strategy will work with the present levels of AMZN. With the market price of $1833.50, the closest money call in the far month will be 1835 strike call. As you write this, it will provide you with a premium of $60.15 for each share. When it comes to the point of determining the long call's strike price, you would like to place this much beyond the closest resistance level. Suppose it happens to be at 1840 level. The overall premium for this be $58.10 for each share. How does the math work?

Trade entry cost = Long call's cost − Premium from short call = 58.1 − 60.15 = -$2.05 (you will earn this on the entry)

Maximum loss = Long call's strike price − Short call's strike price = 1840 − 1835 =$5 each share

Maximum gain = Trade entry cost

The maximum possible gain that you can have from this trade is the premium of the short call. But the long call will also decrease in price simultaneously. So, they will tend to offset each other. As it can be seen, the risk/reward profile is altered for this very strategy, with the risk being much greater in comparison to the reward.

Then, why should someone pursue this? First of all, you will require to understand that the rate of success for this strategy will depend on how well you are able to read the conditions of the market. If the condition of the market is bearish, it will be better for you to purchase a put in place of putting into use the bear call spread. It is the fact that you will be able to generate huge profits in sluggish markets that makes this so attractive in nature.

Adjustment

Is it possible to adjust this kind of trade? The answer is YES. Similar to the bull call spread, in case the market goes in the opposite direction, you can move the spread higher and have the initial legs offset each other either by exercising them or closing them. You can also take the greatest loss and just move on.

Calendar Call Spread

The spreads that we have discussed till now are known as vertical spreads. It implies the way they show up on the chain of options, where the strike prices are properly listed on top of each other. By buying one and shorting another, you will earn the difference between the two. That is why it is termed as 'spread.' Vertical trades will need you to trade the options within the same month of expiry. But in horizontal spreads, which is all about the calendar spread, includes selling and buying the options from various months of expiry. It is a bullish strategy that can be used largely in your favor.

Execution

The strategy of calendar call spread comes with two legs:

- A short term or current month call
- A long term or near month call

The main idea is that when the stock takes time to make itself to the call's longer strike price, you can collect a short call premium in the meantime. The longer call acts as the instrument of profit, which will capture the stock's upward movement.

The longer-term call can either be something from the longer cycle or the near month. The choice will be yours completely. The only thing that you will have to consider over here is the liquidity, as you would not want to trade in an instrument that comes with a huge spread. As long as the spreads are manageable or low, and the liquidity is fine, you will be fine. Let us find out how the math gets implemented with AMZN. Suppose the long call is from the near month. The price that you will pay for the call of 1830, which is the nearest to the market price, is $63.65. For the short call, let's assume there is a medium resistance of 1840. The premium that you will earn on this very call is $36.30.

The entry cost = long call's cost − premium from the short call = 63.65 − 36.3 = $27.35 each share

Maximum loss = Entry cost

There are several scenarios to calculate the maximum profit, as you can actually imagine. It is because it relies on whether the call of the short term ever moves into the money. No matter what the scenario is, you are required to subtract the entry cost from the overall final gain. Thus, horizontal spreads are completely different from vertical spreads because of their open-ended nature.

Chapter 8: Put Spreads

Like the call spreads that permit you to make some good money in every market condition, put spreads will also let you do the same. Most of the traders and brokers prefer using put spreads as there is a lesser chance of any fat finger error, resulting in great risk exposure. For instance, with the strategy of call spreads, if you decide to enter the short call much before even covering the legs of long calls, you will be triggering all types of alarms at the broker headquarter. Is there are any kind of inherent advantage to put spreads over the calls? Well, it will depend largely on the trader type. There are traders who are always hesitant to opt for puts execution. It is because they think a put explicitly gains from a downside movement in the stock where any short call earns only the premium.

It is a very common sentiment among all those who are new to the trading world, and I would like to end such sentiments. There is nothing unethical or wrong in profiting from a downswing. If there is anything, it is only because of economics. If there was no existence of downswings, you would have totally unstable markets. Just like call spreads, put spreads also lend themselves to bearish, bullish, and sideways strategies very well.

Bear Put Spread

The bear put trade tries to take advantage of the bearish markets. In contrast to the bullish markets that come with varying degrees, bearish nature markets tend to have lesser degrees of strength. In simple terms, while a market of bullish nature can be classified according to several levels, ranging from extremely bullish to slightly bullish, bear markets would lend only to three or two such classifications. The reason behind this is quite straightforward. The large majority of institutional activity and the general public are focused only on the long side of the concerned market. So, when such institutions try to conduct their campaigns of purchase, you can notice a greater degree of fluctuation within any specified stock as it rises up. The fact that several traders are always involved in producing more scenarios of price behavior and all these results in a larger number of trend level strength.

In contrast, bearish markets involve far lesser traders. You will never find a bear market opting to make up its mind when it leans towards going downward. Distribution movements, which generally occur before a trend of the bear, do not last long. Bear trends also run faster and exhaust themselves much sooner in comparison to bull trends. The main point over here is that you will have to be on your own with the bear markets. We have already discussed the bear call spread in the last chapter that takes full advantage of the sluggish points of the trend of a bear. The bear put also aims to do the same; however, there are some differences in the way they try to play out themselves.

Execution

The bear put comes with two legs:

- Long put near or at the money
- Short put below the long out of the money

The main instrument of gain over here is the long put, which will be appreciated when the price of the stock decreases. The aim of the short put is to reduce the cost of carrying long put through the earned premium upon writing it. Let us have a look at AMZN to figure out how it works.

The current trading price of AMZN is 1833.51. Let us assume that the trend of bear in this very stock is going to show some signs of getting slow. It is slowly approaching a strong level of support that is not likely to go past. You can learn the identification signs later. At this moment, try to commit to the memory and also note to refer to them at a later phase. The closest at the money put is the 1835 strike price the near month put, which also has an asking price of $53.80 for each share. It is the long portion of this trade. Now, you will have to determine which level will be the perfect one for short. We have seen that a strong level of support is close by that is most unlikely to get breached. Can you use this as the short level? Let us say that this is at $1800. The starting bid for this very put is $39.85 for each share. The math will work out in this way:

Entry cost = Long put cost − Premium from the short = 53.8 − 39.85 = $13.95 for each share

Maximum profit = Difference between the strike prices of long and short put = 1835 − 1800 = $35 for each share

The maximum amount of loss is equal to the entry cost as the premium changes of both the puts will effectively offset each other. As the price goes up, the long put will go down in price, while the short put will go down as well by a similar rate. Thus, you will get a profit that will offset the overall loss on the trade's long leg. By this point, you must have become familiar with successfully working out the spread trade math. Now, you can also see how the dynamics of the same will work. In regards to adjustment, it will work in the same way with the bear put as it tends to do with the bear call. In case the price goes up and takes the long put out of money, you will have to recheck whether your analysis was perfect or not.

In case you think that it holds, you can opt for closing the short, which can provide you with a profit for offsetting the long portion, which will be closed out as well. Try to establish a brand new spread or just maintain the short at the exact level. Keep a note that you can always close out long put and also go along at a higher rate without even touching the short if you desire to maintain it at the same level. The criterion that you will have to follow is exactly the same as the trades of call spreads. The decision that you will make will rely on the factors of technical analysis that you see and also how well you can deduce conclusions from all of them. You will face one more choice, now that you have gained knowledge of how a bear put functions, would you choose a bear put spread or a bear call spread. Both strategies take advantage of the same market conditions. So, which one would you opt for?

Bull Put Spread

Bull put spreads are quite useful in taking advantage of the sluggish uptrends or even sideways movements with a bit of upward tilt towards them.

Execution

Bull put spread comes with two legs:

- Short at the money or in the money put

- Long out of the money put some levels right below the short

The short put is that leg that tries to take advantage of the price rise. The long put can cover your downside if the market sentiment is in your opposition. As you successfully enter the trade, you will be able to earn the premium from put and have to pay for entering the long put. The only difference between the two is the entry cost along with the maximum profit. Your maximum loss is the direct difference between the strike prices of both the legs. In case the strike price falls and brings the long put into the money, your downside will get capped at that level. So, when you enter this trade, you will get a net credit or money. If you try to compare this with bear put, it is a net debit. In short, you will have to pay money to be in the trade. Let us have a look at an example of AMZN.

The price of the market is still the same. However, in this case, the environment is a bit different. The environment is bullish in nature, which is moving upwards sluggishly. The closest at the money put to short is the level 1835. It will provide you with $53.30 for each share. Let us assume that the level of support is 1800. So, the cost needed to go long will be $40.40.

Entry cost = Long put cost − Premium earned from short put = 40.4 − 53.3 = -12.90 for each share

Maximum loss = Short put's strike price − Long put's strike price = $35 each share

Similar to the bear call, the ratio of reward to risk is altered. If you want to make some kind of adjustments to the trade, the criteria are exactly the same as before.

Chapter 9: Common Mistakes Of Beginners

Options are considered a great tool for trading that provides you with the flexibility to use the same in any market condition. You can use options either for generating income, producing good profits, or hedging risks. However, there are some common mistakes in options trading that are mostly made by beginners as they step into the trading world. If not used in the correct way, options can easily erode all that you have in your account. Even it can create margin calls, which is regarded as the worst-case scenario. So, let us have a look at some of the most common mistakes made by beginners that you will have to avoid for your own good.

Focusing On OTM Options

Out-of-the-money or OTM call or put options are much cheaper in comparison to others. So, the majority of new traders think of them as a great deal. Indeed, it is true in some cases, options are priced all the time in such a way that you can never get a tasty dinner for free. The premium or value of the option as you purchase it will keep decaying with passing time. So, not only the price of the option is required to go above or below the strike price, the same needs to be done before the expiration date as well. In actuality, it might result in being a daunting task for making consistent money with the help of this approach. There are times when OTM options trading is only a form of strategy.

It will be really foolish of you if you get stuck in the trap while thinking that as the price of the option is low, it will be a better deal than others. You will have to assess all kinds of probability to check that the underlying asset's price will not go above the strike price before the date of expiry, depending on past tendencies before you buy OTM options.

No Proper Exit Plan

One of the major mistakes made by beginner traders is that they do not possess a proper exit plan. As you opt for a particular trade, you are expecting to earn some money. But how much? How will you determine that the amount of profit is perfect? If an option is on the verge of expiring worthlessly, is it a better option to sell it off much before? Will it be able to reduce the overall loss? Will you stick to the option until the expiration date? All of these, along with many other questions, are required to be addressed before making a trade. Doing these at the time of making the trade is not at all a healthy decision. You will have to be sure of your profit target by tracking the past security movements. You will have to determine some ways in which you can reduce the overall risk. Also, being sure of when to exit the trade is very important.

Not Being Attentive To Small Gains For The Huge Gains

All of us love to enjoy the feeling of making huge gains in a trade. It is very simple and easy to look at the home run trades. But it is actually harder to earn so. The majority of the time, stocks do nothing, and it is quite tough to determine when any of such stocks are going to make a big explosion. Markets keep changing the percentage points continuously. So, you can say that it is quite easier to earn small returns consistently rather than waiting for the big return. Indeed, making 2% only every week by following a fixed strategy is not at all attractive, like making 20% each week. However, piling up various 2% per week is much better than waiting for a huge return.

You need to note that you are building up your capital slowly when you keep making small gains continuously. It will help largely in producing compound returns. On the other hand, when you lose some big trade, you will keep destroying your capital. Thus, you will reduce all the amount of capital that you have in store to make trades. With passing time, all of this will tend to take a negative shape. It is mainly because it will be harder and harder for you to reoccupy all kinds of losses as the position size will also reduce, resulting from the reducing capital.

Not Paying Attention To Written Options

Writing options can turn out to be an effective way to generate income. It is because you will keep receiving the premium amount upfront while selling the options. Whenever an option expires worthless, you will get the chance to keep the overall received amount. The option premium is the maximum profit amount that you can earn. If the price of the security goes in the opposite direction to you, you will incur some huge loss. What is the mistake over here? The main mistake over here is that the option writer fails to lock up a portion of the premium as they get some chance to do so. If you think of selling options like gambling, you have highly mistaken. Getting into trade with the notion, "I wish my option expires worthless. I will get the chance to have all the premium," is not correct. You will have to get involved actively. You will have to realize the altering conditions. If you are 100% sure that an option is going to expire worthlessly, you can relax and just sit back.

However, if the outcome of an option is unclear to you, it will be better for you to close that position as early as possible. For instance, if you sell out put options at $2 and get out of the trade when the premium is $0.40, you will get the chance to have 80% of the premium that you have earned. It is a better option to keep the 80% compared to losing everything.

Chapter 10: Having The Right Mindset

The trading markets are neither moral nor immoral. To be precise, they are amoral. There is no form of emotion in the markets of trading. So, it will completely rely on you the way you will perceive the market. If your main target is to attain and maintain the successful status of a trader in the long run, it is essential to frame the right mindset. It will help you in observing the trading market from a kind of perspective where there is no existence of emotions. The kind of mindset you will have will be responsible for defining all your reactions as you lose trades and earn huge profits. A trader, who is successful, will never allow his/her emotions to play or interfere with the trading decisions. To achieve that, you will have to develop the right mindset. Regardless of the field in life, you are currently in, having a proper mindset will help you achieve all your goals and desires.

Improving Your Mindset

Improving your mindset is a necessity if you are willing to attain success in the trading world. You will have to follow certain strategies and tips that are simple and easy for doing this properly. You will get accustomed to all of them very easily. If you feel that your trading mindset needs some push for going up the ladder, here are some important tips for you. Learning these will help you to survive in the trading game.

Getting Into The Mindset Of A Trader

Traders can benefit to a great extent simply by approaching the trading market with a calm and relaxed mind. If you already have all the risk management guidelines in the perfect place, you are not required to worry about anything. What can go wrong, possibly? Even if a trade of yours reaches the stop-loss level, it is still not the end of the whole world. The game of trading is all about loss and profit. It will keep going on continuously. Even all those traders who are at the top of the success list have their winning only close to 50% than what you actually think. With a high reward-to-risk ratio, which is nothing but the overall ratio of potential profit or loss that might take place in a trade, you can still have some profit with a winning rate near to 50%.

When you lose any trade, it is not necessary to take it too personally. Trading markets move up and down continuously, every hour, every day. All that you will require to do is to have full confidence in your market analysis. In fact, fixing up a daily morning routine can help you to stay calm and relaxed while trading. Some strategies for improving concentration include waking up early, exercise or meditation, relaxing exercise, etc. The key is not to force your mind on a trade; just allow it to flow at its own pace.

Keep Learning

In this world, there is no definite end to learning. It is among all those factors that can separate successful traders from unsuccessful ones. Even after developing the right mindset, you will need to have some proper foundation of the markets to understand the sudden movements in the market along with the reason behind so. In short, you will have to understand the reactions of the market. There are several types of concepts in the trading world that are worth learning. It will always be for your own good if you can keep learning until you figure out the perfect tools that can suit your needs and style of trading properly.

You can opt for learning by reading a good trading book for one hour every day before going to bed to get a proper insight into all the famous practices of the successful traders. You can also opt for some effective online courses to improve your level of knowledge about the trading market. Just keep learning as much as possible. Learning is the only thing in this world that is never going to harm you.

Maintaining Trading Journal

A superb way to attain the proper mindset of a successful trader is by keeping a trading journal. Trading journals are similar to normal journals. The only difference between these two is that trading journals are all about the trading information that you opt for. It will include journal entries, which can literally cover anything that you think is beneficial for your trades. The common standard entries of the trading journal include your traded currency pair, your entry and exit points, reasons for getting into specific trades, and several other important commentaries regarding the trading market. Just after you successfully close a trade, make it your habit to update the trading journal of the same trade simply by filling up the related entries, along with the loss or profit of that trade. If you want, you can add extra comments as well that you think is an essential insight into the trade performance.

When you make it a habit to regularly maintain a trading journal, you can easily keep track of your trading patterns resulting in trade losses. It might also be that the majority of the trades made by you resulted in a loss. Your trading journal can provide you with the necessary insight about the same.

Following this will help you to improve your trading skills so that losses can be minimized.

Keeping A Note That The Market Of Trading Does Not Owe You Anything

A primary mistake made by most of the traders is to overtrade a market continuously. It is specifically when a trade goes in the wrong direction; there are traders who keep chasing the market to get some trading opportunities. It will ultimately result in huge losses right at the end of the day. It is not how the trading market functions. The trading market doesn't owe anything to anyone. It will help you if you can repeat this idea after waking up in the morning every day. Do not get angry if you lose a trade. Always remember, the trading market does not have emotion of any kind, but you do.

Chapter 11: Psychology Of Trading

You will have to master several skills to be a successful trader in the market of trading. Such skills also include the power to evaluate the fundamentals of the concerned company and also determine the direction of the stock trend. However, no other skill is as important as the psychology of a trader. Having emotion, fast-thinking, and exercising the right discipline are some of the major components of what is collectively known as trading psychology. You will have to understand and keep control of two emotions: fear and greed.

Quick Decisions

The majority of the time, traders have to think quickly and also opt for fast decisions. Also, they need to dart in and out of the related stocks within a short period of time. To properly accomplish all these, you will have to develop a certain presence of mind. You will also need to maintain proper discipline to stick to your set trading plans. You will have to understand the perfect time for booking profits and losses. There is no other option to permit emotions to get in your way.

Understanding Fear

Whenever traders get some bad news regarding a specific stock or about an entire economy, they will have a natural tendency to get scared. Also, they might start overreacting to the situation and might also get the feeling of liquidating all the holdings that they possess. In such a situation, they would like to sit on their cash. They might not be able to gather the required strength for taking any other risk again. As a trader, you will have to properly understand the fear: a natural reaction that gets perceived to a threat. Right in this context, it is a threat to all the potential profits. However, quantification of fear can help. You will have to consider figuring out what you are actually scared of. Also, you will need to find out the reason behind the same. But this entire thinking needs to take place much before the occurrence of the loss or bad news, and not after or in the middle of it.

As you think about your fears properly with time, you will get an idea regarding how you perceive various events in an instinctive way. You will also come to know how you react to all of them. All this will permit you to move away from the emotional responses. Indeed, doing all this is not that easy. However, it is very important for the health of your trading portfolio.

Dealing With Greed

If you ever visit Wall Street, you will find a very old saying: Pigs get slaughtered. It actually refers to the greedy attitude of the investors to stick to a single position for a long time with the motive of winning. It also involves getting every tick in the upward direction of the price. However, within a very short period of time, the trend just gets reversed, and the greedy nature of the investor gets caught in a huge trap. Greed is not at all easy to deal with or fight over. It is completely based on the human instinct to do better and to get a little more than what you currently possess. As a successful trader, it is of prime importance to understand such an instinct and develop a proper trading plan which is based on a rational way of thinking. It does not involve any whims or instincts.

Developing Rules

It is necessary for a trader to develop a new set of rules and follow the same when the psychology crunch comes into play. You will have to set up various guidelines depending on the tolerance level of the risk-reward ratio. You will have to determine a fixed profit target. Follow this by putting stop loss right behind it to move your emotions out of the way. Also, you can also decide which nature of events, whether positive or negative earnings, will trigger your decision to sell or purchase any stock. It will be a good thing for you if you can set certain limits on the highest amount that you can actually win or lose in a day. After you have reached your target, take out all your money, and keep running. If your target of loss reaches its predetermined number, fold up your tent and return home.

Conclusion

Thank you for making it through to the end of the *Options Trading for Beginners*; let's hope it was very informative and was able to provide you with all of the necessary tools you need to reach your goals, whatever they may be.

As you have reached the end of this book, you must have noticed that it has been said many times that trading is not a complicated subject. It is either very easy or very difficult. It all depends on the way you see it. Options trading is just like any other primary form of trading. It involves its own set of strategies and tools that you have already learned from this guidebook. Getting a hold of all such strategies will help you in becoming the master of options trading. So, it can be said that it does not even matter whether you a beginner or an expert in options trading. It is open for all. The only thing that can help you going is to remember that regardless of what happens in the trade, never stop learning.

To guarantee a constant flow of income, along with financial stability, options trading is the most effective and safe form of trading. The target of this book is to help the beginner traders with all the basic strategies and tools so that they can also start making profits from the same.

Finally, if you found this guidebook useful in any way, a review on Amazon is always appreciated!

Remember to follow Gualtiero Favole on Amazon to not miss the next books in publication.